Alain Erlande-Brandenburg
Emeritus Conservator General of Heritage

Rouen

Photographs by Jean-Paul Gisserot
Translation by Angela Caldwell

Éditions Jean-Paul Gisserot

www.editions-gisserot.eu

CONTENTS

1 CATHÉDRALE
2 Abbatiale Saint-Ouen
3 Église St-Maclou
4 Saint Patrice
5 Saint-Godard
6 St-Nicaise
7 Église du lycée P. Corneille
8 Église Sainte-Jeanne d'Arc
9 Aître St-Maclou
10 Palais épiscopal
11 Tour Jeanne d'Arc
12 Palais de justice
13 Hotel de Bourgtheroulde
14 Gros Horloge
LA SEINE
HÔTEL DE VILLE
Jardin de l'hôtel de ville
Place du Général de Gaule
Place de la Pomme d'or
Conservatoire national de région
Avenue de la Porte des Champs
Boulevard de l'Yser
Place du Boulingrin
Square A. Maurois
Musée des Antiquités
Chapelle St-Louis
Rue Louis Ricard
Place de la Rougemare
Musée le SECQ des tournelles
Place Restout
Musée de la céramique
Square Verdrel
Musée des Beaux-Arts
Rue Jean Lecanuet
Place du 19 avril 1944
Espace du Palais
Bibliothèque
Monument Juif
Place Maréchal foch
Place des Carmes
Rue Jeanne d'Arc
Boulevard de la Marne
Place Cauchoise
Saint-Romain
Place du Vieux Marché
Musée Jeanne d'Arc
Musée Pierre Corneille
Place de la pucelle
Temple St-Eloi
Place Martin Luther King
Square St-André
Théâtre des Arts
Place des Arts
Quai du Havre
Quai de la Bourse
Quai Pierre Corneille
Rue du Gros Horloge
Place J. Lelieur
Rue Grand Pont
Place de la Cathédrale
Rue du Général Leclerc
Place de la Haute vieille tour
Place du Gaillardbois
Halle aux toiles
Place de la Basse vieille tour
Place de la République
Rue de la République
Place Barthélémy
Place du lt. Aubert
Rue Alsace Lorraine
square Guillaume lion
Place Saint-Marc
Place du 39e R.I
Saint-Vivien
Place St-Vivien
CHU Charles Nicolle
stade Thuilleau
Gambetta
Place du Canada
Hôtel de région

HISTORY

The chevet on St. Ouen's Church.

The origins of the town of Rouen are still shrouded in mystery. Not until the days of the Roman occupation is there known to have been a town at the confluence of the rivers Seine and Robec. It was called Rotomagus and it lay on the right bank of the river, in exceptionally beautiful countryside set within a circlet of lush green hills.

The town was surrounded by walls on the orders of Rome and reduced to 25 hectares within a rectangular enclosure containing four gates. Christianity took hold here very early in the town's history and, after the Edict of Tolerance (313 A.D.), it became a religious centre. A set of episcopal buildings was immediately erected and these constructions have recently been uncovered close to the junction of the north/south (Cardo) and east/west (Decumanus) thoroughfares crossing the town. From the 11th century onwards, Rouen enjoyed spectacular development as the capital of the new Duchy of Normandy. The old town lay within a new 90-hectare enclosure stretching to east and west to include St. Ouen's Abbey and to the north to encompass the very busy suburb of Bourg l'abbé. In 1204, after the fall of Château Gaillard, the town passed into the hands of the Capetian dynasty. Philip Augustus ordered the building of Bouvreuil Castle and the Joan of Arc Tower which is still standing. The population is known to have included 8,000 homes, or approximately 30,000 people. Expansion continued westwards with a Dominican convent until the town became so vast that, in 1346, Philip VI ordered its enclosure within walls and a moat. Their layout can still be seen on plans from the Classical era. The end of the Hundred Years' War marked the beginning of a period of prosperity during which a number of significant public and private buildings were erected and a whole new town, Le Hâvre de Grâce, came into being in 1517. The town developed very little after that and it kept the mediaeval appearance so admired by the Romantics until fairly recent times. Victor Hugo described Rouen as "the town of a hundred bell towers". The town walls were demolished and the moat removed because they could no longer contain a town undergoing rapid expansion. There was a move across the Seine to the left bank, with the construction of four stone bridges in the 19th century. On the right bank, new straight streets were created, providing a panoramic urban vista quite unlike the industrial views on the south bank. The Second World War razed to the ground the town that had inherited more than one thousand years of history. Yet despite all the dramatic events in its past, the town still provides an outstanding panorama of architectural and artistic styles.

The Butter Tower on the cathedral.

RELIGIOUS BUILDINGS

1 NOTRE-DAME CATHEDRAL

The first cathedral

The Gothic building stands on the site of two earlier cathedrals, reflecting the role played by the town of Rouen in the earliest days of Christianity. Recent archaeological digs have revealed traces of the first cathedral built by Bishop Victrice in 393 A.D.

The cathedral of the first millennium

Work began on a new building circa 1,000 A.D., ordered by Archbishop Robert (989-1037), one of the sons of Duke Richard (d. 996 A.D.), and completed by Archbishop Maurille. It was consecrated in 1063. It was a gigantic building, 103 metres in length. It had a nave and side aisles, the West Front projected to the position it has today, the vast transept had an apsidal chapel in each of the arms, and there was an apse flanked by an ambulatory with three radiating chapels that were higher in level than the nave. The cathedral serves as an exceptional reminder of the rebirth of great mediaeval architecture, marked by the use of stone and projecting colonettes. The West Front was flat, and narrower than the one we see today. Inside, the building was very plain; it had its roots in the architecture developed in the 4th century by Constantine's architects with thin walls designed to bear the weight of rafters above (it was 11.50 metres wide in the nave) and numerous doors and windows to bring light in and provide flow between the various areas. The most unusual feature was the chevet with its ambulatory and radiating chapels.

The Gothic cathedral

In 1140, Archbishop Hugh of Amiens, who was probably impressed by the architectural revival referred to by the word "Gothic", wanted to modernise the cathedral built in the millennium. He commissioned St. Romain's Tower which projected 6 metres beyond the alignment of the north wall. Shortly afterwards, in 1140, the West Front was rebuilt with three doorways of which two (St. Stephen's and St. John's) still exist. It was probably circa 1200 that work began on building the redesigned chevet. A massive extension was added to the east side, to include within a single space the canons' choir and the sanctuary. Its roof was also lowered to bring it into line with the roof in the nave. It was at this time that the millennium crypt was demolished and filled in. Work continued with the

The vaulting in the nave of the cathedral.

The elevation in the nave of the cathedral.

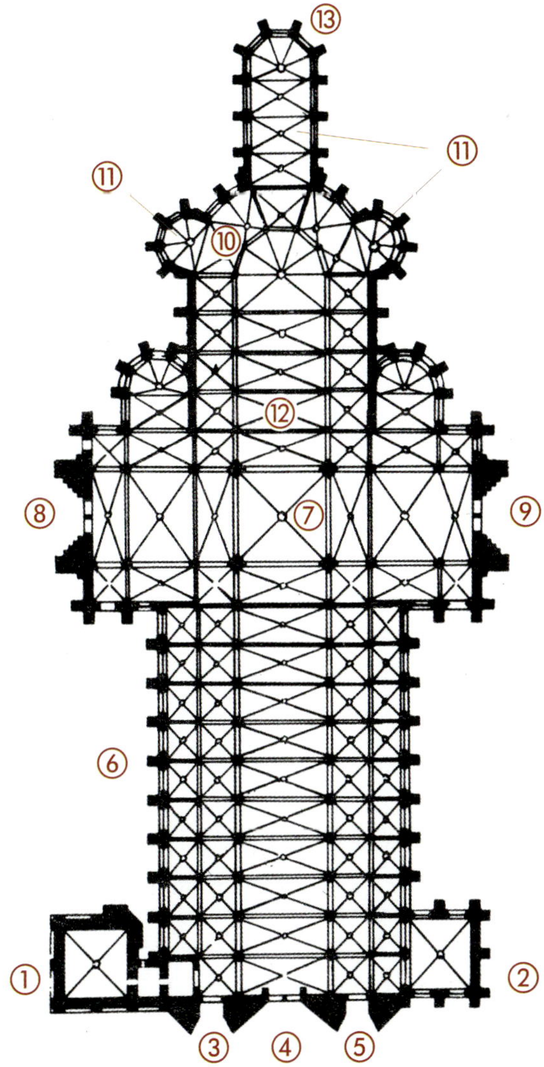

Plan of the cathedral

① St Romain Tower
② Butter Tower
③ St. John the Baptist Door
④ St. Romain Door
⑤ St. Stephen Door
⑥ Cloister (unfinished)
⑦ Lantern tower
⑧ Door in the north arm of the transept
⑨ Door in the south arm of the transept
⑩ Ambulatory
⑪ Radiating chapels
⑫ Canons' choir
⑬ Lady Chapel

St Stephen Door.

The West Front of the cathedral with the St. Romain Tower on the north side and the Butter Tower on the south.

The exterior

The West Front

The size and decoration of the West Front makes it the only one of its kind in France. It is the result of alterations that produced a harmonious if diverse piece of work. At the north end is ***St. Romain's Tower*** ① on which building began in the mid 12th century; at the south end, the ***Butter Tower*** ②. Work began on it in 1485 to designs by Guillaume Pontifs and was completed in 1507 by Jacques Le Roux with a terrace added after fierce argument between those who wished a platform and those who preferred a steeple. The wall stretching between the two towers contains three doorways. From north to south they are the ***St John the Baptist door*** ③ dating from the mid 12th century with a tympanum dating from the middle of the following century and a marvellously elegant carving of Salome dancing; the ***St. Romain door*** ④ dating from the early 13th century (it has since been removed) and, finally, the ***St Stephen door*** ⑤ built at the same time as the one on the north end. Above the doorways is a vast set of architectural features designed to house a group of huge late mediaeval sculptures. To preserve the sculptures, some of them have been moved inside the church. From 1508 onwards, Roulland le Roux was commissioned

transept and its magnificent tower (circa 1237), followed by the sculpted doorways in the transept, the chapels laid out within the piers of the side aisles, the Lady Chapel (1302) which replaced the radiating chapel on one side, the west rose window (1370), the sections at the top of the West Front and the clerestory.

The cathedral witnessed a number of dramatic events - a hurricane in 1683, the French Revolution, a fire in the steeple in 1822, an air raid on 19th April 1944 and a storm on 26th December 1999. After each of these catastrophes, work was undertaken to give the cathedral a new type of beauty, with the Butter Tower standing proud.

The St. John the Baptist Door on the West Front of the cathedral.

The West Front of the cathedral.

to rebuild the central doorway flanked by two piers. Between them he erected a vast pointed gable that covers part of the rose window.

The ***cloister*** ⑥ was erected in the 13th century on the north side of the cathedral. It was never completed and remains the chapter house. The 13th-century ***lantern tower*** ⑦ above the transept crossing was renovated after the fire of 1514 to include a certain number of statues. The steeple rising to a height of 151 metres was recast in iron by Alavoine. Access to the ***door in the north arm of the transept, the Booksellers' Door*** ⑧, is via the Booksellers' Courtyard and a double arcade. Its vertical design was inspired by the doorway in the south arm of the transept in Notre-Dame in Paris, with a steep gable, bays and a rose window also topped by a gable. All that remains of the carving are the two lower lintels depicting the Last Judgement, the coving and the wonderful quadrilobe bases. One of the most moving groups is the Judgement of Solomon on the left pier, purposely placed close to the figure of Christ. Opposite is the ***doorway in the south arm of the transept, the Calende Door*** ⑨, which has a design similar to the one on the north side. The carvings are among the richest of the time, with the tympanum illustrating Christ's Passion. The architecture disappears beneath the monumental sculpture in front of the piers, as it does at the top of the upper gable decorated with the Coronation of the Virgin Mary.

The Calende Door on the south side of the cathedral.

The interior

The chevet

The chevet, or east end, of the cathedral is an admirable blend of tradition and modernity. It retained the millennium layout with ***ambulatory*** ⑩ and ***three radiating chapels*** ⑪ but it then underwent a massive extension eastwards to include the ***canons' choir*** ⑫ with their choirstalls and the sanctuary with the High Altar, all within the same space. It was brought down to the level of the nave by the destruction of the crypt that had raised the previous chevet by 2.50 metres. The contractor integrated modernity into a style that immediately became common among clients and contractors throughout Normandy, with cylindrical pillars, tall capitals, circular abaci, pointed arches and elegant well-proportioned moulding designed to capture the light. The architecture abandoned a four-level elevation in favour of three levels and it gave the blind triforium a certain vibrancy by elongating its designs. The result is admirable. The composition is clear, the spaces are fluid, the designs are rigorous and the workmanship is of the highest quality.

The sanctuary in the cathedral.

The transept

The new transept was designed at the same time as the chevet and was devoid of side aisles so that the extraordinary ***lantern-tower*** ⑦ above the transept crossing could stand on individual supports. Indeed, the building centres on the tower, just as it does in Chartres. When the arm of the transept was built, the radiating décor that was Parisian in origin, was extended along the reverse side of both arms.

Left : The nave and chancel of the cathedral.

Below : The sanctuary in the cathedral.

The cathedral. *Left* : the chevet and steeple.
Right : the transept crossing and lantern tower.

The Lady Chapel ⑬

It was built by Jean Davi on the site of the original side chapel at the request of Guillaume de Flavacourt. It was designed to hold the prelate's tomb but it was very quickly turned into a burial place for the Archbishops of Rouen and certain members of civil society. On the left is the ***tomb of Pierre de Brézé*** (d. 1531), Minister to King Charles VII and Governor of Normandy; only the niche remains. The ***tomb of Louis de Brézé*** (d. 1465), Grand Seneschal and Governor of Normandy, has two tiers. On the lower tier is a skeleton with a depiction of his wife, Diane of Poitiers, at its head; above, in a niche, is the Seneschal wearing full armour and seated on a horse. It was commissioned by Diane of Poitiers, possibly from Jean Goujon. On the right is the ***tomb of the Cardinals d'Amboise***, commissioned in 1509 by Georges d Amboise, Archbishop of Rouen, from Roulland le Roux who carved it between 1516 and

The Lady Chapel in the cathedral.

The cathedral, *left* : the sanctuary.
Right : the western spans in the south end of the nave.

1521. The Archbishop's nephew, Georges II, decided to have it altered in 1521 to leave room for his own statue. The base is topped by two kneeling figures in prayer. The most attractive one is the figure of George I, carved by Pierre des Aubeaux. This group is one of the earliest examples of Renaissance sculpture in France.

The stained-glass windows

Despite major destruction, the cathedral still has one of the most outstanding sets of mediaeval stained glass anywhere in France. As usual at that time, the installation of the stained-glass windows mirrored progress on the building work. The oldest, set in the side aisles, date from the first years of the 13th century. They include illustrations of the ***Life of St. John the Baptist*** and the ***Legend of the Seven Sleepers of Ephesus***. They are typical of the style prevalent in and around 1200, with their wet drapery. A second set, dating from between 1220 and 1240, illustrate the ***Life of Job*** and the ***Life of St. Nicholas***. They were moved from their original position when chapels were built between the piers and are now located among the "Fine Stained-Glass Windows", with some of them in the ambulatory. The less uniform style leaves plenty of space for the use of grisaille. Guillaume de Flavacourt commissioned some major architectural work in 1278, followed by commissions for stained-glass windows i.e. the ***rose window in the north arm of the transept*** and the ***Lady Chapel*** where the elegant style characteristic of the 1300's is more evident. Work in the ***side aisles led*** to major commissions for Guillaume Barbe between 1459 and 1485. He is thought to have had his own company. The main features of this work are the contemplative expressions, the half-shut eyes and the use of beautiful brilliant glass.

The tomb of Richard the Lionheart in the cathedral.

❷ Saint-Ouen

The original building

The Basilica Church of St. Peter founded in the Merovingian Period outside the old town wall was renamed in honour of St. Ouen (or Owen) in the 10th century. The bishop's body, buried here in 684 A.D., quickly became the object of popular worship and this led to the modification of the original name.

The Romanesque building

Abbot Nicholas, son of Duke Richard II of Normandy, began rebuilding the original church circa 1056. It was consecrated in 1126. All that remains of this building is the Romanesque apsidal chapel integrated into the north arm of the Gothic transept. It was known as the ***"Monks' Tower"*** ①; one of its main features are its two storeys of bays.

Layout of the basilica church

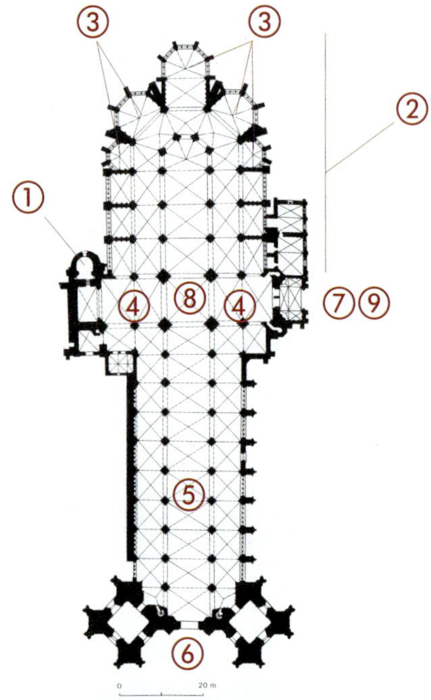

St. Ouen's : the external south elevation.

The Gothic church

On 25th May 1318, Abbot Jean Roussel, alias Marc d'Argent (1318-1339), launched a rebuilding project which he entrusted to an architect who has remained anonymous. It was a gigantic project, of an ambition rarely seen. The cross shaped layout had an unusually long ***chevet*** ②, three straight bays, ***five radiating chapels*** ③ decreasing in size from east to west, an unusually wide ***transept*** ④, an unusually long ***nave*** ⑤ with 10 bays and, finally, a ***West Front*** ⑥ with towers set at an angle to the wall. The project was eventually completed, with the exception of the West Front on which building was interrupted by the French Revolution.

The front was completed between 1845 and 1851 by an architect named Grégoire, who designed a graceless, flat façade that was far removed from the original project. Moreover, the abbey church has one feature that is highly unusual in Normandy – it has no lantern tower. As to the elevation, it consists of the three storeys that were fashionable at the time, with a lit triforium.

St. Ouen's : the rose window in the south arm of the transept.

A built flooded with light

The building is unusually light. The architect reduced the supports to create a skeleton construction and allow the largest possible openings (wide arches and windows) to allow air to circulate and flood the interior with light coloured by the stained glass. The close links between triforium and clerestory consisting of projecting mullions along the interior of the wall and areas of glass pushed outwards have created chiaroscuro effects of a subtlety rarely seen. The design of the windows is also part of this search for delicacy and elegance. The slender lancet windows support one or more rose windows. The work was completed very quickly during the abbacy of Jean Roussel and had reached the transept by the time he died. It then ceased and did not begin again until the early 15th century, under the direction of architect Alexandre de Berneval until his death in 1441. Among other things, he was responsible for the superb ***rose window in the southern arm of the transept*** ⑦. Cardinal d'Estouteville's appointment as abbot in 1462 relaunched the project. Antoine Bobin (1492-1515) continued the nave and had the windows positioned in the vaulted sections. Cardinal Cibo completed the work with the West section of the nave, leaving the West Front unfinished.

Furnishings in St. Ouen's

They include the ***engraved tombstone of Alexandre de Berneval and his son, Colin,*** who was not actually buried in St. Ouen's, and the tomb of another anonymous architect that is admirable for the depiction of a master builder with his costume and the implements of his trade. The ***beautiful wrought-iron grilles closing off the chancel*** were by Nicolas Flambart.

Stained-glass windows in St. Ouen's Church

With its ***eighty stained-glass windows***, St. Ouen's is a remarkable example of mediaeval glass. The layout was defined at the start of the building work and the installation of the windows began with the Lady Chapel. Builders continued to comply with the layout and the design that combined the architectural décor and the damask backgrounds with narrative scenes on the lower section. The work of the first artists was reminiscent of the early 14th-century courtly style seen in Paris and the influence of illuminations from manuscripts was predominant. Their work is recognisable for their dazzling technique. The glass was blown onto large tables, the lead was very skilfully positioned and the faces and drapes were delicately painted. The stylistic changes that appear closer to the West Front do not impinge upon the overall uniformity. The installation of the windows was completed by 1545-1550.

Despite all the stops and starts, the clients and contractors respected the original designs. The differences can only be seen after a very careful analysis of the building. The ***chevet*** ② is part of Norman tradition during the Romanesque period. The masses of stonework are seen as individual features and are superimposed with rare elegance until they end in the tower above the ***transept crossing*** ⑧ with its Flamboyant decoration. The verticality is contrapuntal and highlighted by the piers and double row of flying buttresses. In the south arm of the transept, the so-called ***"Marmousets' Porch"*** ⑨ topped by the old cartulary and the amazing rose window built by Alexandre de Berneval is part of a design frequently seen in this region. It is admirable for the quality of the architecture and the carving of its tympanum dedicated to the Virgin Mary.

St. Ouen's : the transept crossing.

St. Ouen's : the sanctuary.

St. Ouen's 1 : the elevation in the nave. 2: the central tower. 3: the 19th century West Front by Grégoire. 4: the south arm of the transept.

❸ Saint-Maclou

The original church

The parish church dedicated to St. Maclou (Malo or Maclovius) stands between the rivers Robec and Aubette. It became part of the town when the new wall was built. This was the church used by drapers, dyers and leading families of merchants. It collapsed in 1432 and a decision was taken to totally rebuild it.

The new church

Architect Pierre Robin was commissioned to define the general layout and design the various details. Work began in 1436 but continued only slowly until 1476. The church was finally completed in 1521 and was then consecrated. A few additions were made at later dates e.g. the vestry and the main doors including the North door in 1552. Jean Goujon is thought to have been responsible for the two marble columns supporting the organ loft behind the West Front.

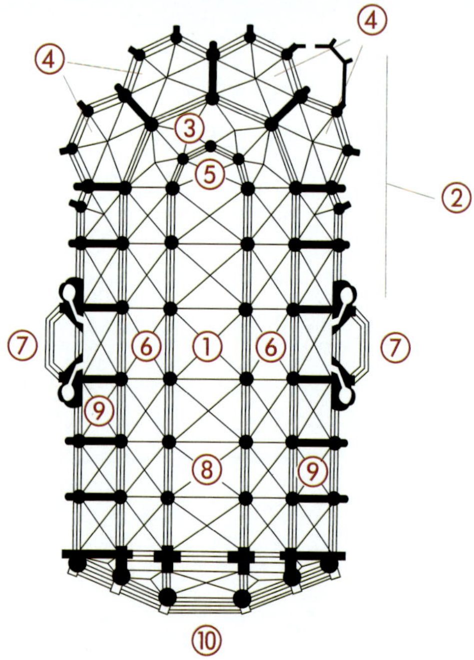

Plan of St. Maclou's Church

The layout is very unusual. It centres on the ***transept crossing*** ①. At the east end, the ***chevet*** ② has two spans and a shallow apse surrounded by an ***ambulatory*** ③ with four identical ***radiating***

St. Maclou's: the marble column carved by Jean Goujon.

St. Maclou's: the vaulting in the nave.

chapels ④, each of them very wide and separated from the others by an internal pier. The eastern chapel lies in line with the ***apse*** ⑤ beyond the column in the apse. Because of this, there is no room for the usual side bay. On the north and south sides are the non-projecting ***arms of the transept*** ⑥, each consisting of two spans and opening to the exterior by a ***doorway flanked by a staircase turret*** ⑦. On the west side is the ***nave*** ⑧ consisting of three spans with side aisles and *chapels* ⑨ set between the internal piers. As to the ***West Front*** ⑩, it is protected by a trapezoidal porch.

The elevation is no less unusual, not because of the three storeys but because of the blind triforium. The architect made unusually skilful use of stereotomy in the prismatic moulding on the pillars, and the arches that are supported directly on the columns, with no capitals. The masterpiece is the lantern tower which, inside and out, gives the building its full meaning. On the outside, it confirms the role of the parish church within its district. Pierre Robin designed a building that stretched upwards to end in the tower above the transept crossing, providing unity for the architectural mass by drawing the eye up from ground level. The gables, flying buttresses and gable end underline an irresistible upward movement accentuated by the various features in the stonework such as the central doorway, the gable end and the tower on the West Front.

The décor, which is sometimes described as excessive, was designed to give gthe stonework a more ethereal appearance and to create a dynamic through a set of transoms and shafts that continue up to the tower. In fact, originally they could also be seen in the wooden steeple which collapsed in 1735 and was replaced between 1868 and 1871 by a new one built of stone.

The sanctuary in St. Maclou's Church.

Stained-glass windows in St. Maclou's Church

Stained-glass windows in St. Maclou's Church

The stained glass was, as usual, made as work progressed but unfortunately the plans were changed over time. Originally, the figures in the lower sections of the windows illustrated legends but most of them have disappeared or exist only in the form of fragments. ***Only window no. 20 has retained its original appearance.*** As was customary in the 14th century, silver yellow was used with grisaille. The upper windows are more colourful.

St. Maclou's : The Passion Window, no. 114, made circa 1470-1505.

Other churches

❹ **Saint-Patrice (St. Patrick's)** is a parish church founded in the 13th century but rebuilt on the same spot from 1535 onwards. The work halted between 1560 and 1648 but was completed in the 19th century. It is a modest building with three aisles and three apsidal chapels containing stained glass from the earlier church as well as a second series of windows commissioned for the replacement building. There are also other stained-glass windows from old buildings in Rouen. The most beautiful date from the Renaissance period and include thirteen windows, the most outstanding of all being the Passion Window in the central apsidal chapel.

❺ **St. Godard's Church,** built in the 16th century, is a hall church with a timber barrel-vaulted roof. The stained-glass windows in the apse are dedicated to the Virgin Mary and are exceptionally beautiful. *The Rod of Jesse* is thought to have been made by Arnoult of Nijmegen, a Dutch glass painter known to have lived in Rouen between 1503 and 1513 and to have supplied numerous designs for windows.

❻ **The church dedicated to St. Nicaise** was rebuilt in the interwar years. It includes a very fine stained-glassed window depicting the Virtues (1555).

❼ **The church in the former Jesuit school** (now a senior high school) has only one aisle, as is usual in Jesuit churches. The nave has five spans with side chapels and ribbed vaulting. The West Front is equally characteristic of Jesuit design with its statues of St. Charlemagne and St. Louis. The names of Father Derand and Father Martellange have been linked with this building.

St. Joan of Arc's Church : the Crucifixion Window, no. 11, donated by Jean de Colbic, 1520-1530.

I·N·R·I

❽ **The Church of St. Joan of Arc (Sainte-Jeanne d'Arc)** stands on the site of the old St. Vincent's Church, which was bombed on 30th May 1944. It was decided that the compensation received after the war would be allocated to the building of a new church and, after much discussion, that the stained-glass windows from the previous church would be installed in it. The architect, Arretche, designed a very daring construction on the very spot where Joan of Arc was burnt at the stake, including the thirteen stained-glass windows that were made in two workshops between 1520 and 1530, as work progressed on St. Vincent's Church. The most famous and most outstanding is the window made by the Le Prince family from Beauvais. Engrand made the window with the chariots. The technique is dazzling thanks to the use of glass and the silver yellow that allowed so many contrasts. All the windows were made in Beauvais by Jean and Engrand Le Prince and transported to Rouen. The second workshop, which made the other windows, was local.

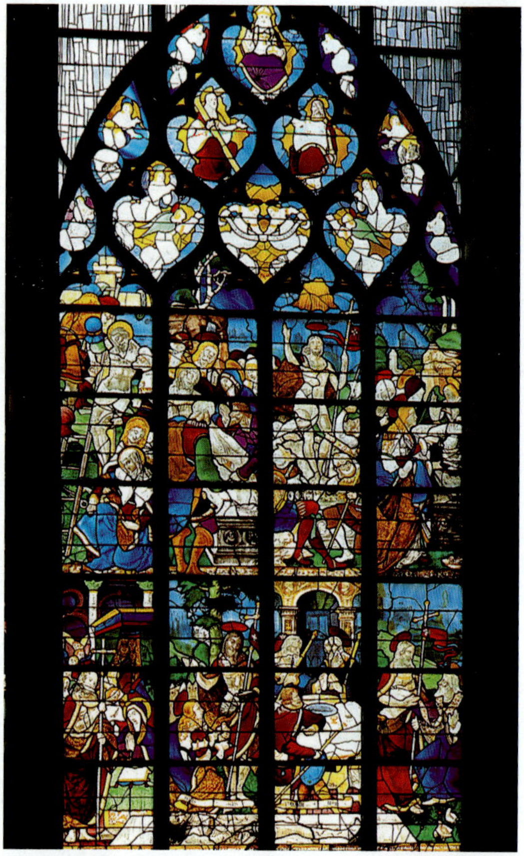
St. Joan of Arc's Church : the Passion Window, no. 10, circa 1520-1530.

St. Joan of Arc's Church.

VERNACULAR BUILDINGS

Close-up of the St. Maclou cemetery.

9 St Maclou Cemetery

This is the old parish cemetery. It consists of a vast courtyard containing common graves, lined on three sides by wooden galleries (originally there was no upper storey) designed to house chapels and funeral monuments. The galleries were later roofed and an upper storey was added.

10 The bishop's palace

Rouen Palace was the traditional urban residence of the Archbishop; Gaillon was his country retreat. Throughout its history, the palace has undergone continuous alterations.

A corridor connected the cathedral and palace.

The oldest sections date from the Romanesque era and include a vaulted chamber. Guillaume de Flavacourt (1278) launched a rebuilding project and a few traces of this have survived. Cardinal d'Estouteville and Georges of Amboise gave the palace a luxurious appearance further enhanced by the addition of a garden inspired by the ones in Italy, with a fountain. No less significant work was undertaken in the 18th century with the building of a new chamber and alterations to the previous one so that it could be used to hang paintings by Hubert Robert.

The Saint-Maclou cemetery.

The Joan of Arc Tower.

⑪ The Joan of Arc Tower

This is all that remains of the new urban layout given to the town after Philip Augustus' conquest of Normandy in 1204. It used to straddle the town walls. The engineers selected the northern site so that the tower could keep a watchful eye on the entire town down in the valley. They copied the Louvre Tower in Paris (1190) in layout, diameter (15 metres) and external and internal features – two gates, one facing the town, the other facing the countryside, a full 7-metre base and a chamber on the ground floor with ribbed vaulting. The internal layout is also common for its day – a niche containing the well, a fireplace, and a spiral staircase in the thickness of the walls leading to the latrines. The upper chamber has a wooden floor. Like its counterpart in the Louvre, the tower was surrounded by a moat that had to be crossed by anybody coming from the royal palace. The upper section was rebuilt in 1840 to plans by the architect Grégoire.

The Law Courts overlooking the courtyard.

⑫ The Law Courts

The land on which the Law Courts were built in the late Middle Ages was known as the "Jewish Enclosure" (Clos aux Juifs). It was confiscated in 1306 by Philip the Fair, a sovereign still remembered today. The site remained unused until 1429 when the herb market was transferred there. In 1499, Louis XII decided to set up Normandy's Exchequer in the merchants' chamber then under construction and it was quickly given additional significance by the building of the Grand Chamber. It immediately became known as the Royal Palace. Other buildings were added to the nucleus, creating an impressive ensemble by the eve of the French Revolution. Modifications, alterations and the Second World War completely changed it. The façade of the Great Parliament Chamber overlooking the courtyard is the most notable section of the building with its eight spans separated by piers aligned with the small central tower. It runs along a length of 66 metres and is

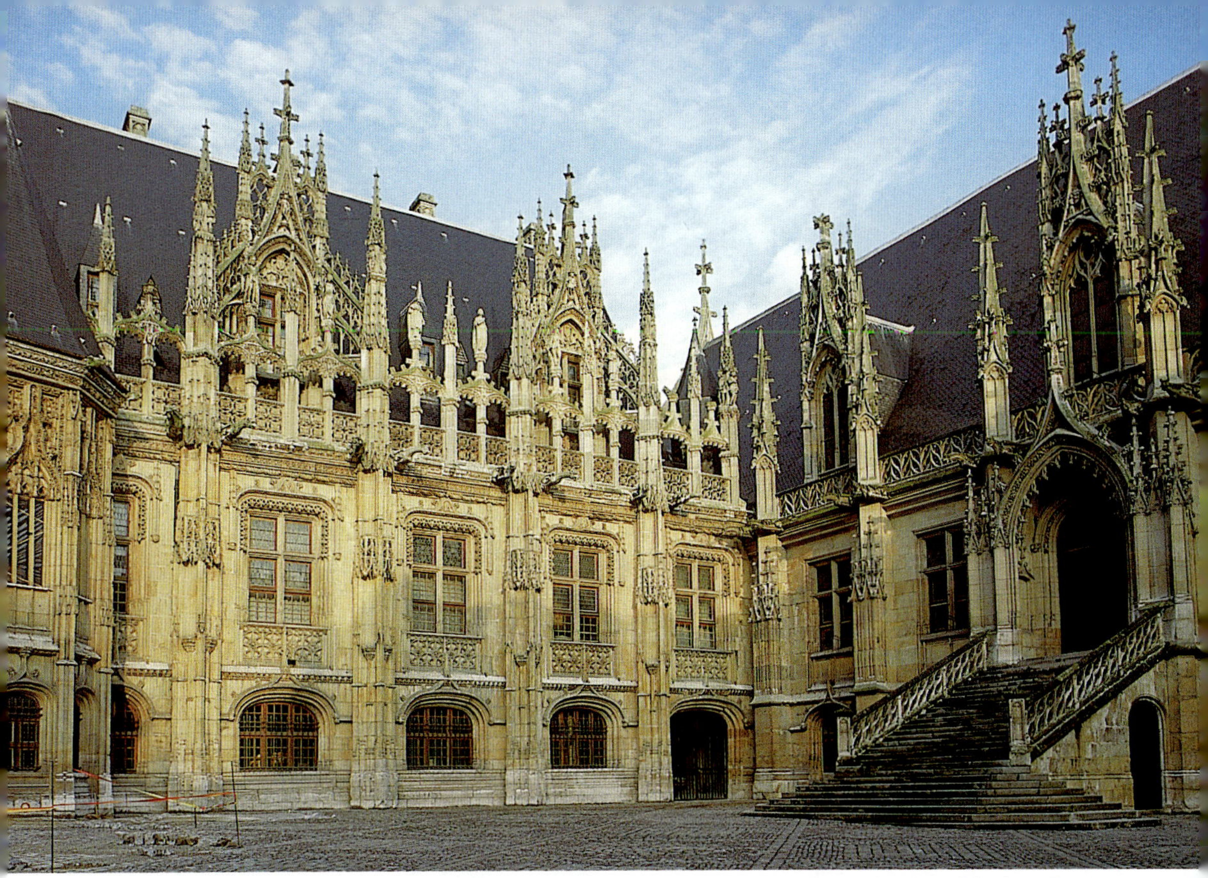

The main wing of the Law Courts.

the finest example of vernacular Flamboyant Gothic architecture in Normandy. The Grand Chamber on the upper floor once had a famous caisson ceiling that was restored in the 19th century. It was destroyed during the Second World War. It was attributed, with some justification, to Roulland le Roux.

The Law Courts overlooking the courtyard.

The dormer windows on the Law Courts.

The Bourgtheroulde Mansion.

⑬ THE BOURGTHEROULDE MANSION

The Bourgtheroulde Mansion is the most representative example of vernacular architecture during the Renaissance period in Rouen for its architecture and its no less superb decorative sculptures. It was commissioned by the aristocratic Le Roux family, several of whom were members of Normandy's Parliament. It was Guillaume II who launched the building on the site of the Calf Market, now Place de la Pucelle, in 1501. The work was continued by his two sons, Claude and Guillaume III alias Father d'Aumale who took part in the negotiations for the Concordat signed by

A mythological triumph.

The meeting of King François I and King Henry VIII.

King François I and the Pope and in the Meeting of the Cloth of Gold between François I of France and Henry VIII of England in 1520. The main section of the building is the urban mansion overlooking the street. It consists of an inner courtyard flanked by three buildings and opening onto a garden. Work began with the two buildings set at right angles to each other on the north and west sides. It continued with the raised open gallery on the south side. In the south-east corner there is a spiral staircase running to the upper storeys. A turret was built opposite it. The Aumale Gallery dates from after the 1520's. It was famous from the outset for the low reliefs on the outside depicting the Meeting of the Cloth of Gold and the triumphs of Petrarch. There are also some decorative carvings dating from the early Renaissance, inspired by engravings in Milan. These carvings are reminiscent of the ones commissioned by Georges of Amboise in Gaillon.

A turret on the Bourgtheroulde Mansion.

The Bourgtheroulde Mansion.

On 19th April 1944, the residence was badly damaged but it has been skilfully and carefully repaired. In 1991, work began on the low reliefs and they have now regained their original beauty.

West wing of the Bourgtheroulde Mansion.

The face of the Town Clock and the Alpheus and Arethusa Fountain by Jean-Pierre Defrance (1732).

⑭ The Town Clock

The Town Clock is the most outstanding historic monument in the town and, miraculously, it has survived unscathed. In 1527, the town's aldermen decided that the town should have a public clock; it was completed in 1529. The plan involved building an archway over the street and increasing the size of the mechanism to provide passers-by with a certain amount of precise information. Beneath the dial, for example, triumphal chariots move past as the day progresses and different gods can be seen on different days of the week. With them are the signs of the zodiac and illustrations of various trades. People at that time were fascinated with such a sophisticated mechanism but the decoration is equally interesting. The ornamentation on the vaulting beneath the arch is reminiscent of the decoration on the tomb of Louis de Brézé in the cathedral. It seems archaic compared to the decoration on the side closest to the Aumale Gallery on the Bourgtheroulde Mansion.

The face of the Town Clock.

A 15th century house in Rue Saint-Romain.

Rouen's Houses

Nineteenth-century town planning and the dramatic events of the Second World War sounded the death knell for a very large number of old houses which, until comparatively recent times before that, had been built of timber. The choice of timber as a building material was explained by the absence of stone quarries nearby and the lush forests in the vicinity. Added to this was the timber recovered from boats that were broken up. In the 15th and 16th centuries, the layout and building techniques used in the houses were identical. The facades had several floors rising to a low, sweeping gable roof. On the ground floor was a shop wide open to the street, a door opening onto the kitchen and a staircase that was usually a spiral. Sometimes, a second building would be linked to the first one by a gallery. The layout of the upper floors depended on the owner's requirements.

The timbering was built by assembling vertical posts and horizontal beams. The posts rose from basement to top; the beams ran through the building, supported on baseplates mounted on the posts. They support the floors. This very ancient technique was replaced by a new building method in the late 15th century. The cost of posts led to the use of shorter ones which had to be placed one on top of the other

The façade of the Finance Office by Roulland le Roux, 1509.

A close-up of the Finance Office.

Medallions on the Finance Office.

A close-up of the Bourgtheroulde Mansion.

while carrying joists, trusses (horizontal beams) and posts on the upper floors. The walls consisted of a series of vertical components (timbering) positioned between the trusses and two braces on each side. Wide openings were made possible by the presence of mullions. This was the technique used in the 16th and 17th centuries.

The third technique seen in Rouen is unusual for the mortise and tenon joints and coupled load-bearing devices. The posts on the upper storeys and the jetty bressumers were no longer placed one on top of the other; instead, they run through the building, tapering as they fit into the mortise and tenon joints. As to the coupled load-bearing devices, they provided support for the central post by two very long, oblique braces set into the sills above the windows. These systems were used in the 17th and 18th centuries.

Finally, to make more space in the upstairs rooms, corbelling was often used until 1525, when it was banned.

The former Town Hall.

IMPRIM'VERT®

Printed and bound by Pollina Luçon 85
Print no. : L72883
Printed in France